The Eagle and the MOON GOLD

A Fable from the Hmong People

Adapted by Yeemay Chan
Illustrated by Kat Thacker

HAMPTON-BROWN

Opposites

poor   rich

small

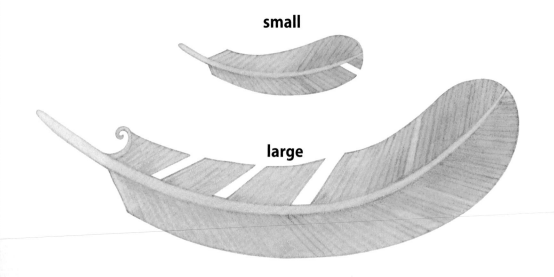

large

few

many

content

greedy

The Eagle and the Moon Gold

One day, a poor boy named Yaoh
went into the forest. He started to
chop down a tree.

Ter! Ter! Ter! sang his ax.

"Stop!" an eagle cried from the sky. "This tree is my home. If you cut it down, my babies will die!"

"I'm sorry," Yaoh said sadly, "I have no choice.
I need wood to build a fire, or I'll die, too."
The eagle thought about Yaoh's words.

Then the eagle said, "I can fly you to the moon. Everyone knows that the moon is made of gold. You'll be rich, and you can buy firewood. Just remember—we must return to Earth before sunrise, or the sun will burn us!"

Shu! Shu! Shu!
Yaoh and the eagle flew to the moon.

Before the sun came up, Yaoh put a few small pieces of gold into his pocket. He was content with what he had.

Yaoh never needed to chop wood again.

Now a greedy man named Gwa lived
in the house next to Yaoh.

Gwa demanded to know how Yaoh got his gold.
Yaoh told him about the eagle and the moon gold.
"I will be rich!" Gwa said to himself.

In the morning, Gwa went to the same tree.
He started to chop.
Ter! Ter! Ter! sang his ax.

"Stop!" the eagle cried from the sky.
"This tree is my home."
   "I have no choice." Gwa lied.
"I need wood to build a fire, or I'll die!"

The eagle said, "I can fly you to the moon.
Everyone knows that the moon is made
of gold."

"You'll be rich!" the eagle added. "You can buy firewood. Just remember—we must return to Earth before sunrise, or the sun will burn us!"

Shu! Shu! Shu!
Gwa and the eagle flew to the moon.

Gwa put many large pieces of gold into his pockets.
"Hurry! The sun is rising!" the eagle cried.
Still, Gwa was not content. He wanted more gold!
More and more! The sun rose higher!
"Too late!" the eagle cried.

Gwa did not listen to the eagle.
He put more gold into his bags.
"We will be burned!" cried
the eagle.

The eagle returned to Earth, but Gwa did not.
He wanted more gold. Then the sun came up!
Gwa and all his dreams melted into the moon.

Moral: Greed robs you of what you already have.